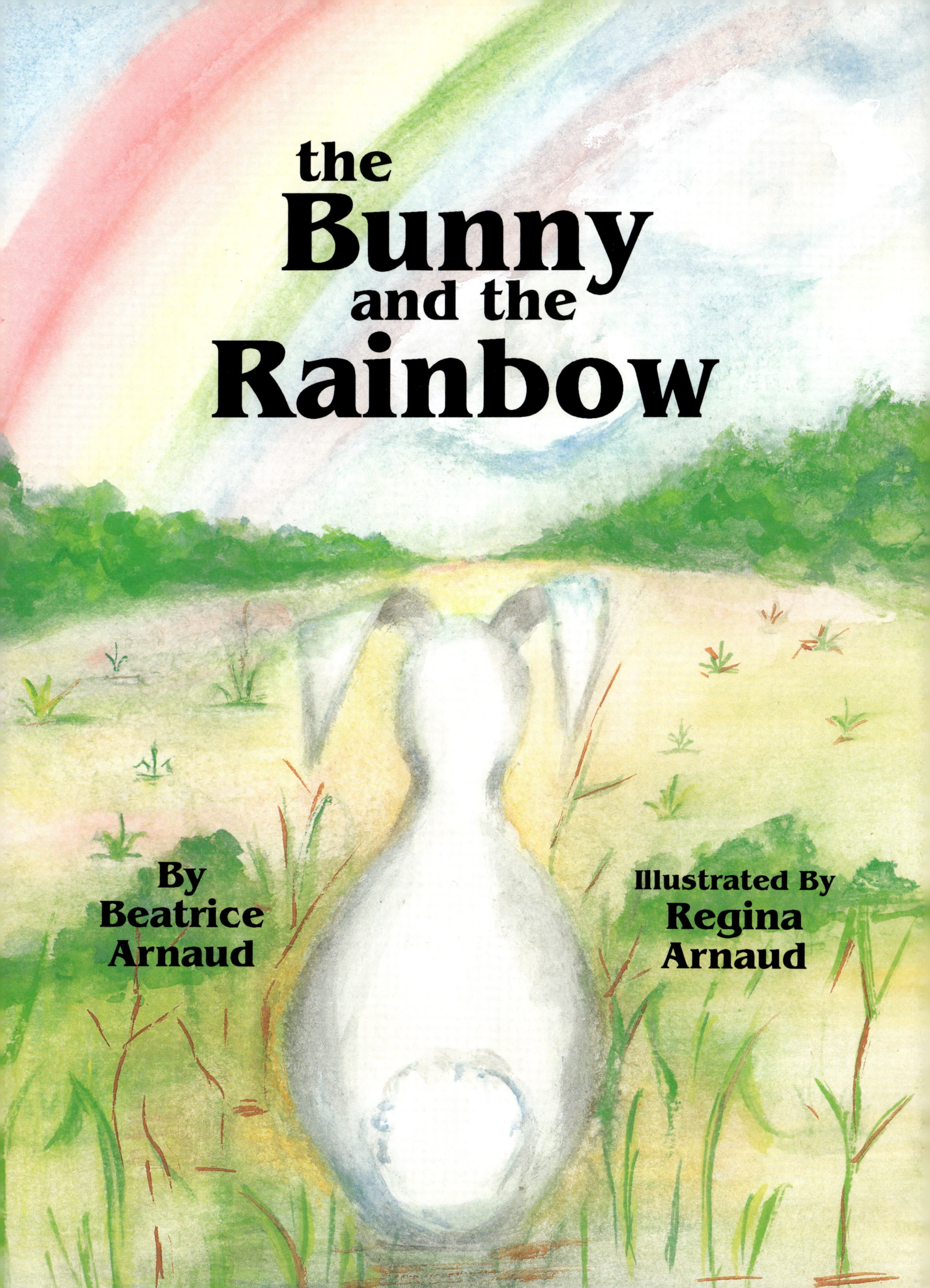
the Bunny and the Rainbow
By Beatrice Arnaud
Illustrated By Regina Arnaud

Printed in the United States of America

Lafayette, Louisiana

To Order Call: 1-888-2 READ LA

Library of Congress Number 96-086008

ISBN 09654468-0-8

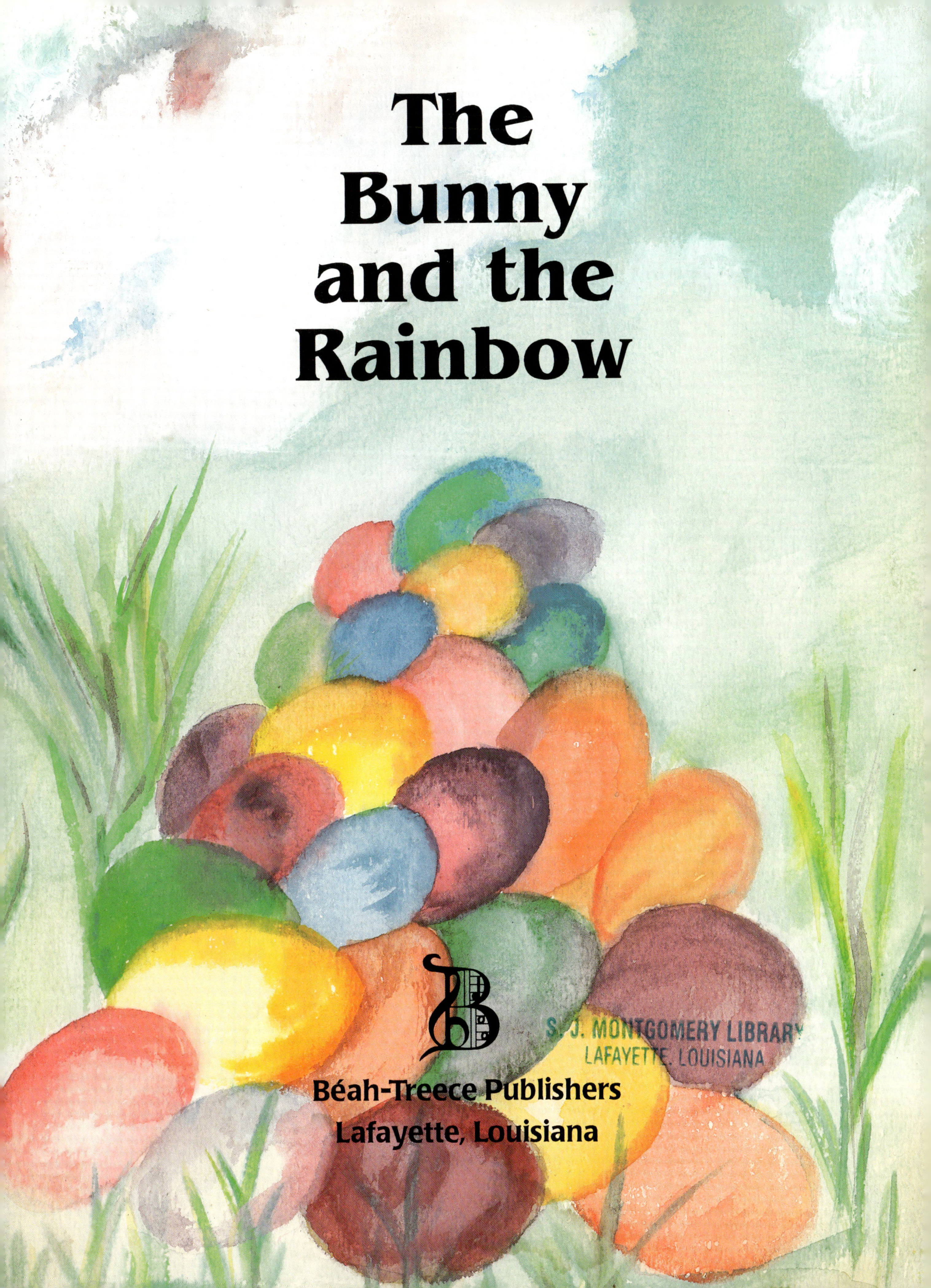

The Bunny and the Rainbow
S. J. MONTGOMERY LIBRARY
LAFAYETTE, LOUISIANA
Béah-Treece Publishers
Lafayette, Louisiana

A very long time ago,
Bunny eggs were white as snow

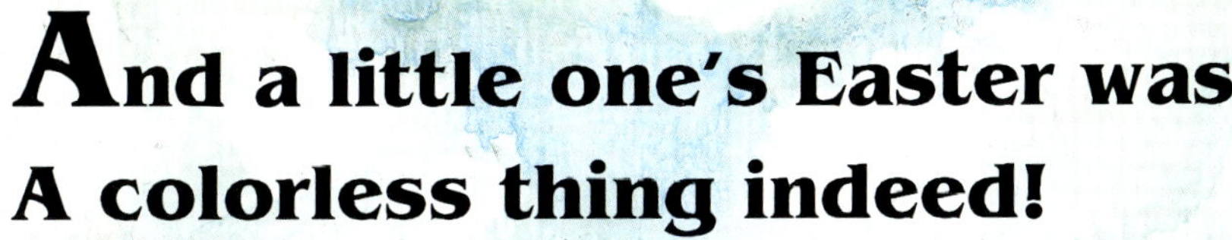

And a little one's Easter was
A colorless thing indeed!

Until one Happy,
Happy Year

PSST"

A Rainbow whispered in a bunny's ear:
"Mr. Rabbit, won't you please take heed?"

"You could give your eggs
that Happy Easter taste ~ ~ ~

By using these colors that I've got going to waste."

So, the Bunny borrows colors from the Rainbow

Just to tint a million eggs
for me and you.

And he does it all alone,

Works his paws right to the bone,

Making eggs all pink...

and green...

and yellow...

and blue.

Yes, the Bunny borrows colors from the Rainbow,

'Cause
no earthly store
has every
heavenly hue!

And he does it all, I guess,

Just to bring some loveliness

And a
Happy,
Happy
EASTER
to You!

Colours from the Rainbow

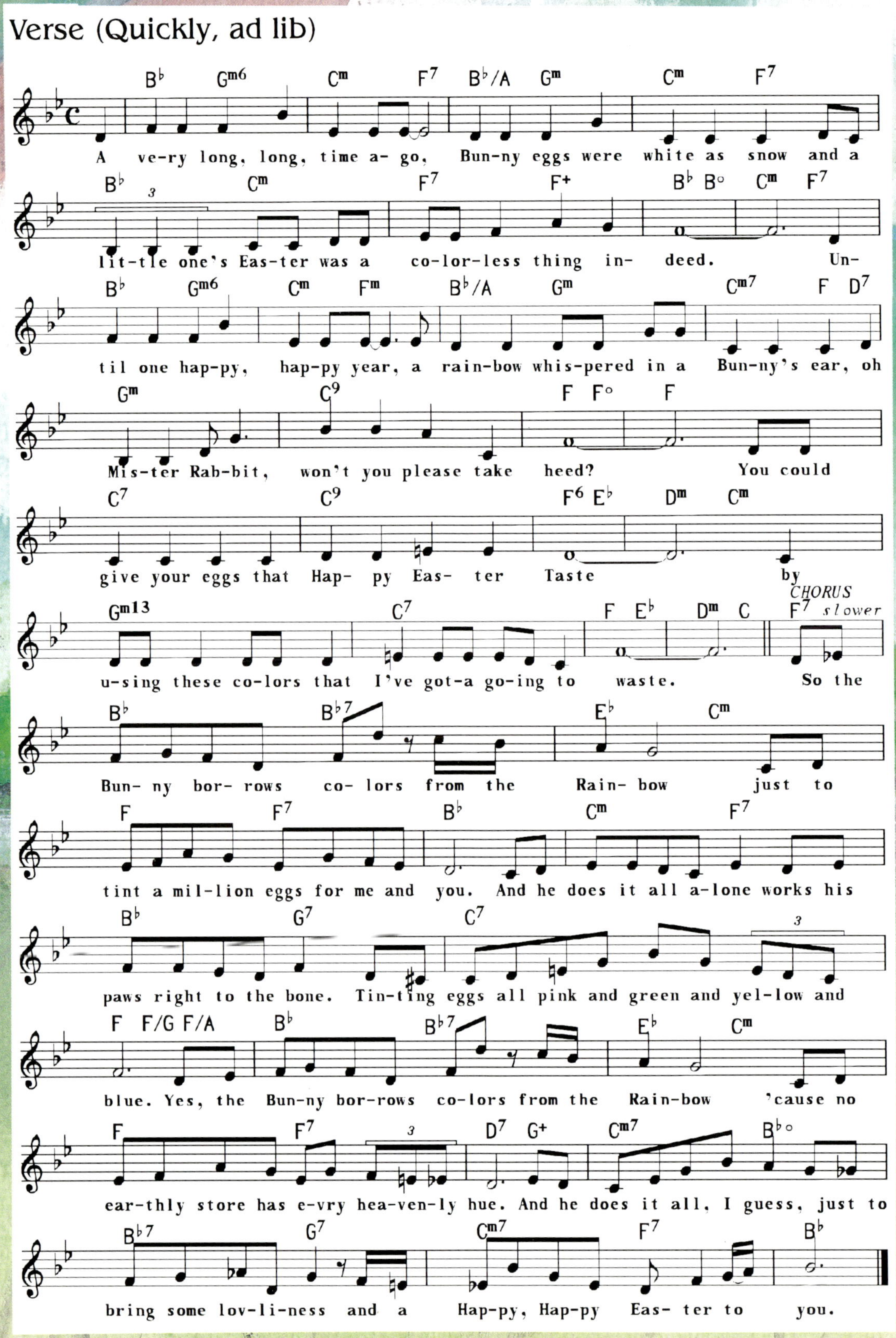

A ve-ry long, long, time a- go, Bun-ny eggs were white as snow and a
lit-tle one's Eas-ter was a co-lor-less thing in- deed. Until one hap-py, hap-py year, a rain-bow whis-pered in a Bun-ny's ear, oh
Mis-ter Rab-bit, won't you please take heed? You could
give your eggs that Hap- py Eas- ter Taste by
u-sing these co-lors that I've got-a go-ing to waste.

CHORUS *slower*

So the
Bun- ny bor- rows co- lors from the Rain- bow just to
tint a mil-lion eggs for me and you. And he does it all a-lone works his
paws right to the bone. Tin-ting eggs all pink and green and yel-low and
blue. Yes, the Bun-ny bor-rows co-lors from the Rain-bow 'cause no
ear-thly store has e-vry hea-ven-ly hue. And he does it all, I guess, just to
bring some lov-li-ness and a Hap-py, Hap-py Eas- ter to you.